GRIM BASTILLES

OF DESPAIR

THE POOR LAW
UNION WORKHOUSES
IN IRELAND

PASCHAL MAHONEY

This essay is part of the interdisciplinary series *Famine Folios*,
covering many aspects of the Great Hunger in Ireland from 1845–52.

CONTENTS

So rattle my bones all over the stones
I'm only a beggar-man whom nobody owns.

Thomas Noel, *fl.* 1846

GROUP OF CABINS AT ARDCARA.

INTRODUCTION

As the funeral cortège in the "Hades" chapter of *Ulysses* winds its way around Rutland (now Parnell) Square, a pauper coffin leaving the Rotunda Hospital prompts some half-remembered lines of verse to pop into Leopold Bloom's head: "Rattle his bones. Over the stones. Only a pauper. Nobody owns." Though Bloom may not have known it, these lines are from a Chartist song written by Thomas Noel in the early 1840s, a period that witnessed the introduction and consolidation of new Poor Laws in Britain and Ireland. Noel's words passed into popular culture, and first became familiar to me through The Smiths's 1984 song "The Hand that Rocks the Cradle". Morrissey's haunting lyric played repeatedly in my mind as I was walking by a high stone wall surrounding a dormer house outside Lismore, County Waterford. I realized that it was once the entrance building of the town's workhouse, where tens of thousands had perished during the Famine. Across the country, hundreds of thousands had died in identical workhouses, having been forced through eviction and starvation to abandon the wretched living conditions of their mud-and-straw hovels – "the abodes of extinguished hope", as the journalist N. P. Willis put it:

I did not know that men and women, upright and made in God's image, could live in styes like swine, with swine – sitting, lying down, cooking and eating in such filth as all brute animals ... [in cabins so poorly built that there was] no bar ... to the liquid filth that oozes to its lower reservoir within (Belfast Journal, July 19, 1845).

The fate of the destitute poor prompted further reflections on the circumstances that brought about these buildings, about how they functioned, and the effect they had on the lives of those who lived, worked, and died within their walls. This short study focuses on these grim edifices that once dominated the outskirts of many Irish towns.

Figure 1 | "Group of Cabins at Ardcara" (*Pictorial Times*, January 31, 1846)

AN ENGLISH SOLUTION FOR AN IRISH PROBLEM

On January 11, 1839 George Wilkinson, a twenty-four-year-old Englishman, arrived in Dublin to begin the largest architectural public commission yet undertaken in Ireland. Over the next fourteen years the construction of his workhouse buildings and the implementation of the Irish Poor Laws were to have a profound impact on the physical and cultural landscape of the island. By April 1847 all planned 130 workhouses were complete. However, the catastrophic failure of the potato harvest in 1846 increased the numbers of destitute poor to such enormous levels that thirty larger workhouses were built in a second phase between 1849 and 1853.

Ireland in the 1820s, with a population of about 6.5 million, was one of the most densely populated countries in Europe. A great percentage of the Irish population lived in dire poverty, leading the French writer Gustave de Beaumont to comment in 1839 that "In all countries paupers may be discovered, but an entire nation of paupers is what never was seen until it was shown in Ireland" (35). The great majority of these poor survived as small tenant occupiers ("peasants", to use the popular term), but increasing numbers became migrants, wandering from town to town, begging and seeking seasonal labor, thereby causing the British government to become greatly concerned about the spread of disease and the growing numbers of destitute people emigrating to Britain, which, by the 1830s, "had reached deluge proportions" (O'Connor 52).

The appallingly high number of Irish poor was a long-term consequence of the British policy of plantations in Ireland, where the land of the native Irish had been usurped and handed over to a small number of landlords loyal to the Crown. The displaced population was reduced to subsistence tenant farmers, who – in the words of contemporary observer Asenath Nicholson – would serve these landlords as

a race of people who would dig their ditches, build their walls, lay out their parks and ponds, for a penny or two a-day, and above all, could be made patiently to feed on a single root, and live in mud cabins, or by the side of a rock, or burrow in sandbanks, who would "go at their command, and come at their bidding" and beside, for the unleased patch of ground, where they grew the root on which they subsisted, they paid such a rent as enabled the masters of the soil to live and fare sumptuously at home, to hunt the hare and deer over the mountain and glen, with lady, dog and gun, or to travel in distant lands (84).

Ireland was not alone in dealing with the problem of destitute poor. The English solution, in the form of Poor Laws, had established a legislative and administrative system where parishes could combine to form a "union" to build workhouses that would provide relief and work for the poor. This system was extended to Ireland in 1838 through the Act for the Effectual Relief of the Destitute Poor in Ireland, with the country being divided into 130 unions. Each union was to set a Poor Law rate to finance the building and administration of its workhouse. The governing principle of the system was that the relief given at public expense should be less than that which could be gained from physical exertion outside. In order to limit the number of those entering the workhouses, the regime of life within was designed to ensure that nothing short of absolute destitution would compel anyone to seek refuge there. The effectiveness of this policy of dissuasion was reflected by the fact that up to the Famine most workhouses were less than half full.

The workhouse system can, at best, be seen as an honest attempt to deal with the rising problem of pauperism, which was attributed to the indolence and primitiveness of the people themselves rather than to the accelerated modernization of agricultural improvement and industrialization in Britain, a process encouraged by government policies of the time. The Irish Poor Laws were to be more severe than those in England, as the poor in Ireland would have no legal right to relief, and no able-bodied man would receive relief unless he entered a workhouse, so ending all existing systems of outdoor relief. This was to have a disastrous effect during the Famine, as the union guardians no longer had any obligation to fund alternative relief or accommodation. It was also significant that the numbers to be accommodated in each Irish workhouse was to be higher than those in England, highlighting the greater scale of pauperism even before the Famine.

The inauguration of the workhouse system in Ireland was solidly resisted by the many who supported alternative recommendations to provide relief through the undertaking of large-scale public works. However, these proposals were rejected by the British government, and in July 1838 the workhouse system was introduced with the passing of the Act for the More Effectual Relief of the Destitute Poor, one of the most despised Acts ever to come into effect in Ireland, and which led Daniel O'Connell to comment, "What is now suggested is that a country unable to give employment to its labourers should be made to feed them in idleness within the walls of a poor-house."[1] This view was also shared by the American writer Asenath Nicholson, who observed in the account of her travels across Ireland, *Annals of the Famine in Ireland, in 1847, 1848, and 1849*, that

The unreclaimed bogs and waste hunting grounds tell, that in no country are poor-houses such an anomaly as in Ireland; and the Irishman who is willing to work, and is employed there, has no moral right to be either grateful or satisfied that he has exchanged even a mud cabin of liberty for a palace walled and locked, where his food is measured and doled, where his family are strangers to him, and all the social interchanges of life are taken from him wholly. Though a man may be "a man for a' that," yet he cannot feel himself one; nor does he seldom, if ever, regain that standard of manly independence which belongs to man, whatever his future lot may be (84).

The Irish were not the only critics of the workhouses; many in England also questioned the morality of the system. Most famously, in *Oliver Twist* – generally appraised as a harsh criticism of the workhouse system – Charles Dickens described the inmates of English workhouses as "offenders against the poor-laws" who would be housed "without the inconvenience of too much food or too much clothing" in buildings that he cynically imagined the guardians considered to be "brick and mortar elysiums" (11). In truth, many of the advocates of the workhouse system were solely interested in the process of further detaching the peasant from the land

by offering to the poor man a sure prospect of a maintenance in case of absolute need, to loosen his hold upon the land and thus relieve the landlord from the incubus which now presses upon him of restoring to the landlords the power of doing what they will with what they own (O'Connor 63).

The workhouses were in reality detention centers in which the inmates were guilty of no crime other than the poverty imposed by the policies of the British government. The paupers had no more freedom than state prisoners, their liberty was withdrawn, and family members were prohibited from communication with one another other than "a few hasty moments one day in seven". In *Annals of the Famine in Ireland*, Nicholson wrote that

they are prisons under a different name, calculated to produce a principle of idleness, and to degrade, never to elevate, to deaden in the human heart that rational self-respect which individual support generates, and which should be kept up; and may I never be doomed to die in a poorhouse (85).

The already stark conditions in the workhouses deteriorated rapidly over the course of the Famine, and as the fate of the poor darkened, the fear of confinement rose, heightening the horror associated with the workhouses in the Irish psyche. In total, an estimated 370,000 people died in workhouses during the Famine years, and for those who survived and for the generations who followed them, the experience remained deeply traumatic.

The extensive written records and minutes of the Boards of Guardians and the Poor Law Commissioners provide useful insight into the running and management of workhouses, but tell little of the plight and daily existence of the paupers. Photography was in its infancy during the Famine, and no contemporary photographic images exist; nor were the voices of the inmates recorded to tell the real story of their miserable existence within the cold stone walls of the buildings. However, the imposing structures of the many surviving workhouse buildings provide a physical context for helping us reconstruct and imagine what life was like for the inmates during those tragic years. Some buildings – including the workhouses at Donaghmore, County Laois and Portumna, County Galway [Figure 2] – are being preserved by committed groups of local historians, and it is hoped that at least one will be fully restored to provide a tangible and permanent reminder of the indescribable suffering that once blighted this island.

Figure 2 | Portumna Union Workhouse

Figure 3 | Ramsay Richard Reinagle, *Sir George Nicholls*

DESPICABLE ACT

Ireland is like a half starved rat that crosses the path of an elephant. What must the elephant do? Squelch it, by heavens, squelch it (McCabe 73).

In 1833 the First Royal Commission for Inquiring into the Condition of the Poorer Classes in Ireland was established. It was chaired by Richard Whately (1787–1863), archbishop of Dublin. In some respects he was an unlikely choice, for though he was to the forefront in promoting "political economy", he was considered to be a radical and unsympathetic to the prevailing Benthamite and Malthusian ideologies of the time. Whately's understanding of the Irish character led him to believe that the English workhouse system would not work in Ireland. He assessed Ireland's poverty to be different to that of England: the Irish were poor, he said, "not out of indolence or a reluctance to work" but because "there was no work on the island for a class of people, whose numbers were overwhelming in comparison to the wealthy few who provided the employment" (qtd. in Burke 284). His comprehensive report, which took three years to compile, was presented to Parliament in May 1836. It recommended an enlightened system of poor relief based on public-works projects to be funded by state loans and local rates. However, the report was poorly received by the government, which considered it too out of line with its more extreme utilitarian and laissez-faire economic views. Instead, a second Royal Commission of Inquiry was established, this time chaired by George Nicholls (1781–1865) **[Figure 3]**, a Poor Law legislator and one of the key objectors to Whatley's report. Nicholls was known to share the Malthusian and Benthamite views of the British government, and was a champion of the workhouse system, believing in its moral and social benefits. Whatley was aware of Nicholls's views, and remarked after hearing of his appointment that "I do not say that he is not right in this: I can only foretell that he will come back with the conclusion because he took it out with him and is not likely to lose it on the way" (qtd. in Quinn 34).

The philosopher Jeremy Bentham (1748–1832) had written extensively on the management of the poor, and promoted the establishment of workhouses. His idea of spatial segregation of the different categories of inmate (male/female, adults/children, infirm/able-bodied) was a key principle of the system. Segregation was considered to be a practical and economical way to house and manage the poor, and also served as a punitive measure to dissuade the masses from seeking relief. His detailed proposals for the management of workhouses incorporated his views on the kind of food to be provided and his calculations as to the maximum number of people per dormitory and their sleeping hours. The overall strategy of the workhouses was to draw a major line of distinction between the class of "independent laborers" outside and the class of "paupers" inside these heavily regulated institutions.

Thomas Malthus (1766–1834) had written extensively on population control and was of the view that any benevolence towards the poor was self-defeating. He believed in the necessity of famine as a device for controlling population, and asserted that the poor were sinfully responsible for their own hunger – sins that could only be redeemed through hard work.

Nicholls's report was compiled following a six-week, twelve-county tour of Ireland in 1836, following which he observed of Irish paupers that "The standard of their mode of living is unhappily so low that the establishment of one still lower is difficult" (Poor Law Commission, *Fifth Annual Report* 34). Given the established principle behind the standards of workhouses – that they should be worse than the standard of living endured by the paupers outside their walls – and given, too, that the living conditions of the poor in Ireland were worse than those of the poor in England, it is not surprising that Nicholls proposed a vision of an Irish workhouse even more harsh than his Benthamite image of an English one. Nicholls was not unaware of the Irish dislike of confinement; in his first report published after his initial tour, he observed that "The Irish are naturally, or by habit, a migratory people fond of change, full of hope, eager for experiment. All the opinions which I have collected from persons most conversant with the Irish character confirm this statement. Confinement of any kind is most irksome to an Irishman"(24). He also knew that the Irish poor in England sought to avoid refuge in the workhouses, even as a last resort, and did not remain there if they could obtain any means of support outside. Knowing of this fear convinced him that confinement "would produce such a horror of the Workhouse that nothing short of destitution and necessity would compel anyone to seek relief there, and ensure that they would quit it again as speedily as possible"(qtd. in O'Connor 61).

Nicholls's report was accepted, and in July 1838 – with the passing of the Act for the More Effectual Relief of the Destitute Poor in Ireland – the workhouse system was extended to Ireland. According to the provisions of the Act, 130 workhouses were to be built.

GEORGE WILKINSON, ARCHITECT: "A GOOD MAN, STEADY, ABLE AND LABORIOUS"

In England the system for appointing architects for workhouse commissions was through competition, thereby providing opportunities for architects to improve and expand on the various model plans developed by Sampson Kempthorne (1809–73), architect of the Poor Law Commissioners. Nicholls was concerned that this process would impede the timely delivery of the projects in Ireland, and was determined that a uniform design would be adopted for Irish workhouses. Initially, he planned to retain the architectural services of the Board of Works; however, this proved problematic:

It was first supposed that the Board might be available for superintending the erection of the buildings thus relieving us from the position of the responsibility as well as taking upon itself the chief portion of the onerous duties connected with the fulfillment of the contracts. We were advised however, that there were legal objections to our devolving upon any other body (qtd. in O'Dwyer 56).

Frederick O'Dwyer explains that this legal objection could have been overcome through a simple amendment to the Act; however, there appears to have been no effort in this regard. The Board of Works had been recently established (in 1831) but had limited resources, and it appears that it was reluctant to undertake the workhouse commission due to its enormity. The Board's architect, Jacob Owen (1778–1870), "understood the magnitude of the job and was not keen to extend the vast amounts of energy and travel that he would have to endure in erecting 130 buildings across the country" (Quinn 38). It is also likely that the Board was keen to avoid involvement due to the unpopularity of the Poor Law Act in Ireland.

Nicholls sought proposals from three architects – Sampson Kempthorne, George Wilkinson, and a third whose identity remains unknown; O'Dwyer speculates that the third may have been an Irish architect "who after the furore broke, wanted to remain anonymous", or was perhaps someone nominated by Jacob Owens, "who liked to promote the interest of his relatives" (15). The furor referred to was due to the Irish architectural profession not being invited to compete for the work.

This was by far the largest public-works project in Ireland up to that time, with a budget of approximately £1 million – more than five times greater than any previous commission. The dismay of Irish architects at the appointment of an English architect had the effect of consolidating Irish architects as a group, and led to the foundation in 1839 of an association to represent the profession, the Royal Institute of Architects of Ireland.

Figure 4 | Photograph of George Wilkinson

In January 1839 George Wilkinson, then only twenty-five years of age, secured the appointment to become the Commissioners' architect in Ireland. His selection was based on three principal criteria: first, the strength of his workhouse-design experience in Wales "under circumstances, and with materials not very dissimilar from what exist in Ireland" (Poor Law Commission, *Fifth Annual Report* 57); second, his two standard plans – one for 400–800 inmates and one for 800-plus inmates – met fully the requirements for classification and separation; and third, the building costs were considered to be economic – about a third less expensive than the cost of building the English workhouses.

Nicholls saw in George Wilkinson a practical and somewhat impressionable young architect who would willingly assist in the implementation of his vision for uniform plans **[Figure 4]**. Wilkinson was born in Witney, Oxfordshire in 1814 to William Wilkinson, a successful builder, and Mary Wilkinson; he was the eldest of five sons. The Wilkinsons were a well-to-do family, and known to be hard-working and ambitious. William Wilkinson's successful business laid the foundations upon which "George and his brother William could elevate their status within the building trade to that of architect" (Quinn 15). There is no record of either having had any formal training; rather, it would appear that they learned their profession through participation in their father's building projects in Oxfordshire, not in the Royal Academy and on the grand tour of Europe as enjoyed by gentlemen architects. But as an ambitious young man, George was determined – through hard work, guile, and an affable personality – to overcome the limitations he might encounter in his career due to his status as a provincial architect.

In "Perspectives on the career of George Wilkinson", Beth-Anne Quinn explains that architects were in great demand at the time due to a significant population increase (15). This provided opportunities for provincial architects to secure public commissions previously dominated by their Royal Academy–trained counterparts. In 1835, at the age of twenty-one, Wilkinson won his first public commission – to design the workhouse in his home town (Witney, Oxfordshire). Sampson Kempthorne, a London-based architect who had been the "preferred architect" of the Poor Law Commissioners, had originally been appointed, but his failure to meet deadlines, his non-attendance at meetings, and his disregard for direction had annoyed the Witney guardians sufficiently for them to terminate his contract and transfer the commission to the local architect. Wilkinson's *X*-shaped plan was based on Jeremy Bentham's panopticon design for prisons and other institutional buildings. The main building had a central octagonal hub containing the master's quarters, whose windows provided views in all directions. The four three-storey wings radiating from the center contained the dormitories and day rooms for each of the various category of inmate (male/female, infirm/able-bodied, etc.). A similar design was used in Wilkinson's next commission for the workhouse at Chipping North. The architectural style of these buildings is Italianate (featuring classically detailed columns and arches) with Tudor influences; both styles would have been very familiar to him given that his studio was located in the university city of Oxford, to where he had moved in 1838.

Wilkinson's next workhouse commission, in Thame, Oxfordshire, took a different design approach, introducing a cruciform plan with a central dining hall/chapel. In total, he undertook eight workhouse commissions within a year of his twenty-first birthday, and established himself as a "competent workhouse architect and an inventive and economic planner" (Quinn 33). He made efforts at this time to move away from workhouse design and to gain more-prestigious commissions in Oxford. He was evidently successful in this as he won the commission for Bampton Town Hall in 1838, and in the same year was appointed county surveyor, a position he held until 1841.

Wilkinson was known to Nicholls, who, in a letter to John Shaw-Lefevre (April 8, 1839) seeking support for the appointment of Wilkinson, described him as "a good man, steady, able and laborious".[2] His inclusion in the competition for the Irish workhouse commission was undoubtedly based on his growing reputation as the most economically prudent of the workhouse architects in England. Wilkinson's knowledge and use of local materials, his business acumen, and his frugal approach to building were to become the cornerstone of his workhouse technique. It is likely also that Wilkinson considered the commission in Ireland – where few architects would have been formally trained – to be an opportunity to elevate his position within the profession and to raise his status in society.

The Commissioners' brief for the Irish workhouses stated that "The style of the building is intended to be of the cheapest description compatible with durability; and effect is aimed at by harmony of proportion and simplicity of arrangement, all mere decoration being studiously excluded" (Poor Law Commission, *Fifth Annual Report* 59). It was clear that the model Irish workhouses were to be of an even meaner character than Kempthorne's English versions.

Figure 5 | George Wilkinson, Bird's eye view of workhouse to contain 400 to 800 persons

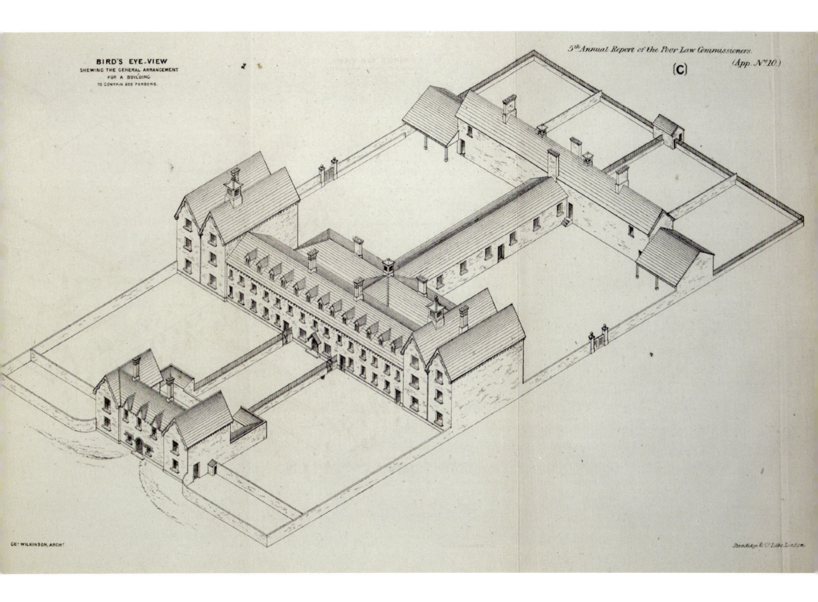

BIRD'S EYE-VIEW
SHEWING THE GENERAL ARRANGEMENT
FOR A BUILDING
TO CONTAIN 800 PERSONS.

G⁰ WILKINSON, ARCH.T

Standidge & C° Lith. London.

MODEL PLANS: THE WINNING DESIGN

Wilkinson's designs – which delivered the physical manifestation of the ideological thinking of the Poor Laws "through the use of uniformity, spatial segregation, ceremony and symbolism" (Thomas 156) – were successful, and on January 11, 1839 he arrived in Ireland to take up position of architect to the Irish Poor Law Commission, with responsibility for the design and erection of all 130 Irish workhouses. He was to be paid an annual salary of £500, and provided with a full-time assistant and a clerk, to be paid £150 and £100 per annum respectively (Poor Law Commission, *Fifth Annual Report* 57). This was a substantial saving for the Exchequer compared to the standard commission in England of 3.5 per cent of construction costs (Quinn 45). Wilkinson's roles were to complete the design of the buildings (each capable of holding from 300 to 1,300 inmates) **[Figure 5]**, tendering the building contracts, inspecting sites, investigating availability of local materials, and designing and overseeing the procurement of all fixtures, fittings, and furniture.

Wilkinson set to work on the vast building program, preparing standard plans that could be slightly modified to suit local circumstances. The plans were published as an appendix in the *Fifth Annual Report of the Poor Law Commissioners* (1839). Two versions were illustrated, one accommodating 400–800 inmates, and one for 800-plus; both were capable of expansion to provide for an additional 200 inmates. The standard designs were presented in the report in the form of a ground-floor plan and a bird's-eye isometric view. The proposed style of the buildings was Tudoresque, which Wilkinson described as "the least obtrusive: while its gabled roofs and elevated chimney shafts give it a pleasing and picturesque appearance" (Poor Law Commission, *Fifth Annual Report* 134). The application of an historic style was typical of the time; Wilkinson was a "man of his period; and in the early Victorian period architects chose styles for their association with the past ... Wilkinson chose a style associated with alms-houses – as built in England during Tudor and Jacobean periods, with lots of gables, decorative barge boards, diamond glazing" (Dallat 24). Internally, the detail was to be spartan, with the unplastered walls and raw timber floors and roof structure simply whitewashed to help maintain hygiene.

The basic plan incorporated plain elevations with little decoration to ensure the stringent economy of the buildings and to achieve the fit-for-purpose design required by the Commissioners. However, a separate series of drawings were produced with more-elaborate designs for optional decorative features, such as bargeboards, gates, and ventilation towers, thereby permitting the guardians of each union some limited choice in the design. Nicholls had been of the view that a uniform design would forestall the possibility of local Boards of Guardians rejecting the design and thereby causing construction delays. Despite his efforts, a small number of boards insisted on a more decorative design, most notably for Carlow workhouse, which featured arched walkways and extensive Italianate detailing. However, the standard floor plans remained unaltered **[Figure 6]**.

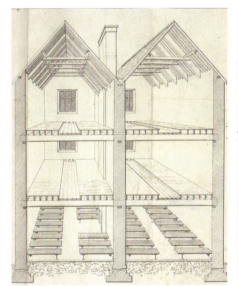 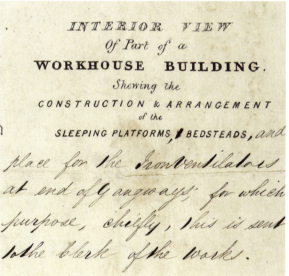

Figure 6 | George Wilkinson, Interior view of the workhouse building, showing the construction and arrangement of the sleeping platforms and bedsteads

Construction of the workhouses instituted an unprecedented scale of building in the Irish rural landscape; prior to this, the modest structures of churches and the occasional mill had dominated. Many of the sites chosen for the location of buildings were on a hill to ensure an imposing presence when viewed from the nearest town, consistent with the Commissioners' recommendation that workhouses should be located "conveniently to the town and in a lofty position" (Poor Law Commission, *Fifth Annual Report* 134). However, the guardians always had the final say as to location, and their decisions were heavily influenced by cost. In *Annals of the Famine in Ireland*, Asenath Nicholson describes an observer coming across a workhouse

after traveling many a weary mile over bog and waste, where nothing but a scattering hamlet of loose stone, mud, or turf greets him, when he suddenly turns some corner, or ascends some hill, and sees in the distance, upon a pleasant elevation, a building of vast dimensions, tasteful in architecture, surrounded with walls, like the castle or mansion of some lord, if he knew not

Ireland's history, must suppose that some chief held his proud dominion over the surrounding country (134).

The guardians running the workhouses were ratepayers themselves, and no doubt were keen to keep construction and running costs to a minimum. Many were also traders or were linked to builders and suppliers, and would have sought to benefit from the associated construction and supply contracts. In several locations the guardians had offered the less costly option of converting existing buildings for use as workhouses; however, the ideology of uniformity overruled that of economy, and almost all were rejected by the Commissioners, who were resolute in their opinion that the principles of the Poor Laws could only be achieved in purpose-built buildings.

The first workhouse – one of the three largest – opened in Cork on March 1, 1840. The rest followed at a steady rate, and in April 1847 Wilkinson reported that all 130 workhouses had been completed. Collectively, they had a capacity to house in excess of 93,860 paupers, with running costs amounting to £12 per head (Poor Law Commission, *Thirteenth Annual Report* 213–19). The design, procurement, and construction of 130 buildings at a cost of £1,145,800 in such a short period of time was an extraordinary achievement in the 1840s given the basic technology available and the travel difficulties encountered, and something that would be difficult to match today. However, one has to wonder if the same expense applied to Whatley's alternative relief of public-works projects would not have yielded a more effective and humane outcome for the destitute. In all, 5,230 architectural drawings were prepared (utilizing large-format, heavy drafting paper). Standard drawings were printed by Forster Lithographic, Crow Street, Dublin, then modified by hand for use on each workhouse project. A significant collection of these drawings are retained in the Irish Architectural Archives, and they show the fine pen work and watercolor techniques of the time. Wilkinson was justifiably proud of his achievement and felt entitled to claim that

no future works are ever likely to be executed at so low a rate of cost as the new workhouses have been. In offering these remarks, I have carefully examined the prices paid for work in new barracks by the Board of Ordnance, as well as other public buildings. I can also say that up to this time I am not aware of any failure in the works that deserves even mention, or from first to last, of even a settlement in the walls of any of the main buildings of the 130 workhouses that deserves such a name (Poor Law Commission, *Thirteenth Annual Report* 213–19).

Wilkinson produced a standard written specification for the buildings in which he described in detail the type of construction and materials to be employed. The specification document was reproduced for each workhouse contract, and sometimes modified by hand with text and sketches to deal with site-specific conditions. In this document Wilkinson instructs that the external walls are to be constructed from

Figure 7 | View to stairs from dormitory, Portumna Union Workhouse

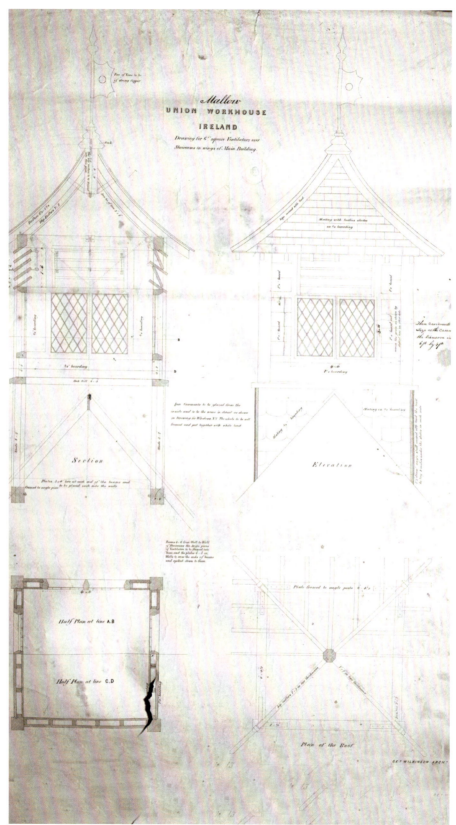

Figure 8 | George Wilkinson, Part of drawing showing detail of ventilator over main stairs, Mallow Union Workhouse

carefully selected local-stone rubble work – generally limestone, granite, or sandstone – with various applications of "rough hammer-dressed wall stones" (Wilkinson, *Specification of Works* 4) for quoins, string course, entrance door architraves, cills, and air vents. The window openings were to be formed with dressed stone or brick jambs, with a shallow arch head in the same material. The windows were to made from cast iron, with the upper casement hinged to fall inside, which would allow the windows to be opened during rainy weather.

The ground-floor surfaces were to be formed with mortar and earth rather than stone (as used in the English workhouses), which Wilkinson justified in the *Seventh Annual Report of the Poor Law Commissioners* as "being less cold than stone and less liable to decay than wooden floors", and better suited to people accustomed to walking barefoot since most of the occupants, it was assumed, "will be without shoes and stockings" (357).

Upper floors were to be constructed from large oak beams – "either Riga, or of Irish or English growth ... or Quebec Red Pine timber" – that would span the full width of a building, and would be supported by profiled stone corbels built into the outside walls. The floors and sleeping platforms were to be constructed from a simple but intricate arrangement of timber joists and one-inch-thick tongued "white American deal" floorboards "left rough on the underside to receive whitewash" (Wilkinson, *Specification of Works* 9).

The plain but beautifully crafted stone stairs were formed by cantilevered stone landings and steps designed "to tail at least six inches into the walls", with simple, square, three-quarter-inch, cast-iron balusters, "the stone steps to the stairs to be rough punched or pecked on the underside, and close punched or pecked on the upper face of the treads, risers and end" (Wilkinson, *Specification of Works* 5) **[Figure 7]**.

The timber king-post roof trusses were to be left open and exposed so as to improve air circulation, with the underside of the slate roof finished with lime parging. Ventilation was a key design concern for Wilkinson, as it was critical to the prevention of the spread of disease – such as cholera and famine fever – in the close confines of the dormitories. The *Fifth Annual Report of the Poor Law Commissioners* included a detailed section on ventilation by Wilkinson in which he described the design of a ventilation tower positioned over the main circulation stairs "containing windows hung at centres, and moveable with a line, to admit any circulation or change of air required" (133). His detailed calculations for the volume of air to be provided in the infirmary ensured 800 cubic feet of air for each individual (partially provided by additional air flues in the chimney stacks) **[Figure 8]**.

Wilkinson also designed semicircular, perforated panels over the doors that led from the stairs to the dormitories, and which, "without producing any strong current, would always effect extensive ventilation during occupation of the rooms" (Poor

Law Commission, *Fifth Annual Report* 133). The standard arrangement for ventilating dormitories in the English workhouses had been the provision of openable windows on either side of a room so as to enable controllable cross-ventilation. However, due to concerns about the spread of disease and the likelihood that the windows would be closed during cold weather, Wilkinson inserted into the walls small flues a few inches above the floor and covered with cast-iron gratings. These would ensure permanent ventilation regardless of the temperature outside, thereby providing well-ventilated but often bitterly cold dormitories.

Heating was basic, with at most one fireplace per dormitory, where a "group of pale sickly-looking children cower about a vast iron guard, to keep the scanty fire that might be struggling for life in the grate"(Nicholson 83), and, more often than not, the only heating generated was the body heat of those who occupied the rooms. The fireplace surrounds for rooms to be occupied by the inmates were to be a simple brick detail; however, more-elaborate fireplaces (to the value of £2) were to be provided for staffrooms, and the most expensive (£4) was to be placed in the boardroom. This grading of finishes was also applied to doors, windows, and other details – all of it consistent with the prevailing classification ideology **[Figure 9]**.

There were two generations of Wilkinson workhouse designs: the first generation, based on the published plans of 1839 – generally referred to as pre-Famine – were constructed between 1839 and 1849. The apparent simplicity of the plan disguises a complex and technically inventive arrangement of the various functions so as to achieve the level of segregation required. The second-generation workhouses were built between 1849 and 1853.

Figure 9 | George Wilkinson, Section drawing through dormitory building, Portumna Union Workhouse

Portumna   Union Workhouse.

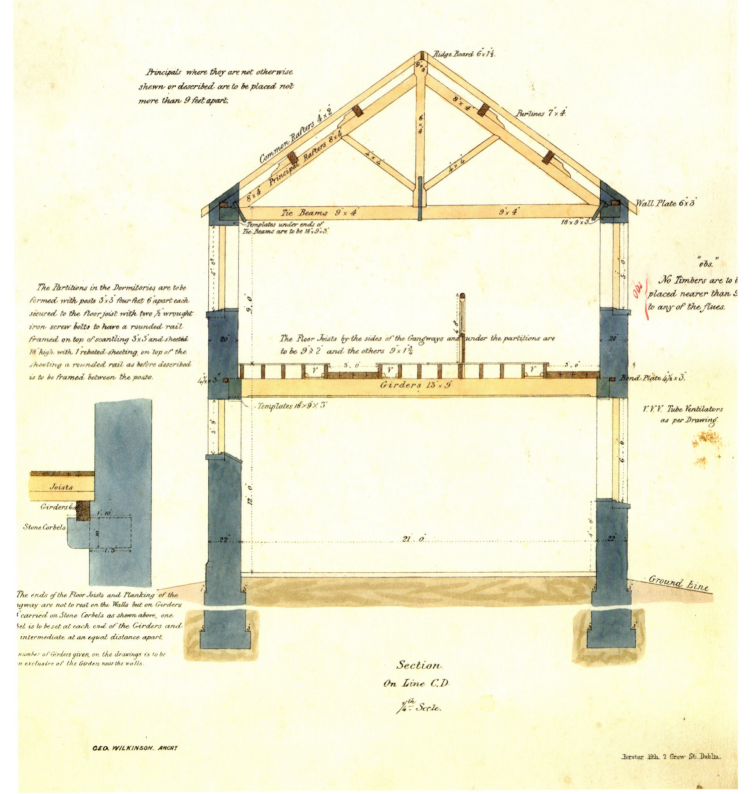

Principals where they are not otherwise
shewn or described are to be placed not
more than 9 feet apart.

Ridge Board 6 × 1½

Common Rafters 4 × 2

Principal Rafters 8 × 4

8 × 4

Purlines 7 × 4

9¾

6 × 4

4 × 4

4 × 4

Wall Plate 6 × 3

8 × 4

Tie Beams 9 × 4

9 × 4

18 × 9 × 3

Templates under ends of
Tie Beams are to be 18 × 9 × 3.

"obs."

No Timbers are to b
placed nearer than 9
to any of the flues.

The Partitions in the Dormitories are to be
formed with posts 3 × 3 four feet 6 apart each
secured to the floor joist with two ½ wrought
iron screw bolts to have a rounded rail
framed on top of scantling 3 × 3 and sheeted
18 high with 1 rebated sheeting, on top of the
sheeting a rounded rail as before described
is to be framed between the posts.

The Floor Joists by the sides of the Gangways and under the partitions are
to be 9 × 2 and the others 9 × 1¼

20

20

4½ × 3

Girders 13 × 9

Bond Plate 4½ × 3.

Templates 18 × 9 × 3

V.V.V. Tube Ventilators
as per Drawing.

Joists

Girders 6 ×

Stone Corbels

1. 10

m

1. 3

22

21. 0

22

Ground Line

The ends of the Floor Joists and Planking of the
Gangway are not to rest on the Walls but on Girders
carried on Stone Corbels as shewn above, one
Corbel is to be set at each end of the Girders and
intermediate at an equal distance apart.

number of Girders given on the drawings is to be
exclusive of the Girders near the walls.

Section
On Line C.D.
¼th Scale.

GEO. WILKINSON. ARCHT

Borster lith. 2 Crow St. Dublin.

PRE-FAMINE WORKHOUSES

The 1839 pre-Famine design shows the buildings arranged in three distinct sections. The first section, or front building, was the public façade of the workhouse complex, presenting a two-storey, five-bay structure where the greatest investment in terms of architectural decoration was made. Situated 150 feet (45.7 meters) in front of the main dormitory building, it contained a boardroom for the guardians as well as a clerk's office on the top floor, with the porter's room, probationary wards, and a gatekeeper's area located at ground level. Positioned either side of the front building but screened behind high stone walls were small exercise yards serving the probationary wards. The privies and fumigation closets were located at the rear of the building, and behind these a narrow garden led to the main dormitory building. On either side of the garden, separated by a high wall, were the boys' and girls' yards **[Figure 10]**.

The front building was where the poor would enter to seek admittance. Upon arrival they would initially be housed in probationary male and female wards located on the ground floor to the left and right of the receiving hall; vagrants could also seek temporary relief here. The provision of probationary wards secured the main wards from the risk of infection by new inmates prior to them being declared free from disease. Here they would be subjected to the "workhouse test" to determine if they were "deserving poor". The clerk would log their details: name, sex, age, townland, religion, and landlord. To prove their destitution they had to agree to sign over any rights they may have had to land or property, and to forgo any claim to the hovels they previously inhabited, "oathing that he owns not either 'hide or hoof', screed or scrawl, mattock or spade, pot or churn, duck-pond, manure-heap, or potato-plot, on the ground that reared him, and simply put his seal to this by pulling the roof from his own cabin" (Nicholson 84).

The medical officer would determine the physical condition of prospective inmates so as to establish whether they were able-bodied or not. Once accepted, they would be issued with tickets of admission. The clothes they wore on entering the workhouse

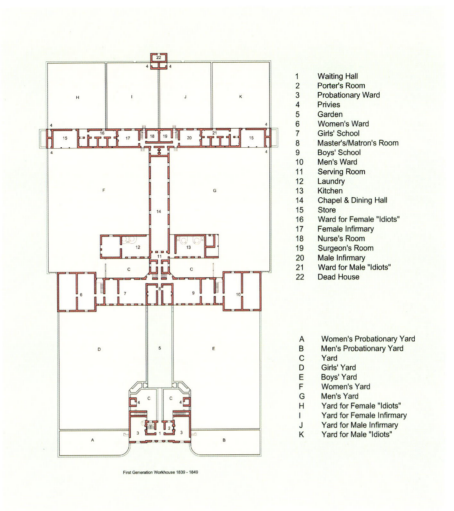

1 Waiting Hall
2 Porter's Room
3 Probationary Ward
4 Privies
5 Garden
6 Women's Ward
7 Girls' School
8 Master's/Matron's Room
9 Boys' School
10 Men's Ward
11 Serving Room
12 Laundry
13 Kitchen
14 Chapel & Dining Hall
15 Store
16 Ward for Female "Idiots"
17 Female Infirmary
18 Nurse's Room
19 Surgeon's Room
20 Male Infirmary
21 Ward for Male "Idiots"
22 Dead House

A Women's Probationary Yard
B Men's Probationary Yard
C Yard
D Girls' Yard
E Boys' Yard
F Women's Yard
G Men's Yard
H Yard for Female "Idiots"
I Yard for Female Infirmary
J Yard for Male Infirmary
K Yard for Male "Idiots"

First Generation Workhouse 1839 - 1849

Figure 10 | Ground-floor plan, first-generation workhouse

were removed, and inmates were washed, fumigated, and provided with penitential-style striped workhouse uniforms (most often manufactured from cloth woven in workhouses), as the prevailing view was that "inmates should be worse clothed, worse lodged and worse fed than independent labourers in the district" (O'Connor 61). They were now deprived of individual identity. The strict policy of segregation was applied, and families were separated and discharged to male, female, boys', and girls' sections. Parents were only allowed to see their children for, at most, a short time each day, and often, during the bleakest years of the Famine, this was the last place mother, father, and children saw each other.

For many, upon realization that hunger and disease had reduced them to a desperate condition, entering the workhouse was a final attempt at survival. During the Famine years, many left it too late. According to one report:

With regret we have to add another name to the melancholy catalogue of the dead from starvation in this district, in the person of an aged poor woman named Mary Commins, who, while on her way on Wednesday to seek admission in the workhouse, expired on the side of the road near Dangan, within about a mile of the town (Galway Vindicator, January 23, 1847).

This had not always been the case: entering the workhouse in the pre-Famine years was certainly a social stigma, but it was a far less severe prospect than during Famine times. In pre-Famine times, many wives and children would enter the workhouse for part of the year while their husbands worked in the seasonal labor force.

The second section of the workhouse complex was the largest building, and contained the dormitories. This building featured a long, two-storey façade with double-gabled three-storey blocks at either end. Women were housed in the dormitories on the left side of the plans and men on the right. Adults, children, and the old were located on different floors. All slept on platforms constructed from timber boards raised above the floor and covered in simple straw mattresses so as to maximize the number of occupants **[Figure 11]**.

The master and matron had ground-floor rooms that opened onto the garden leading back to the front building. The day-to-day management and overall running of the workhouse was the responsibility of the master. He enforced order and ensured that the able-bodied worked. He was also responsible for physical punishment, which was applied through more-onerous labor, confinement in the refractory wards, or

Figure 11 | Dormitory sleeping platforms, Portumna Union Workhouse

whipping. He was also responsible for keeping records, such as the master's journal, as required by the Commissioners. The master's wife usually acted as matron, and ran the female part of the workhouse.

The wings on the ground floor contained day rooms, a nursery, the girls' school on the left side of the plans, and the boys' school on the right. Children, it was asserted, would "benefit from an education that befitted them as pauper children" (Thomas 158). The system of education was based on that operated by the Board of National Education, and the books were the same as those in use in the National schools. The children were taught basic reading, writing, and arithmetic, and received religious instruction. Boys were also taught trades such as tailoring, shoemaking, weaving, milling, baking, and carpentry, while girls were trained in knitting, sewing, embroidery, and laundry services. Boys and girls were taught in separate schoolrooms, with well in excess of a hundred pupils in each. Staffing levels were low: there was usually just a schoolmaster and an assistant in each schoolroom, and often they were not properly trained or qualified. Boys also worked two half-day shifts on the farmland attached to the workhouses, and were given agricultural instruction. This system ensured a constant supply of labor on the farm and a constant number attending school. Outside of school hours the girls helped out with the household chores.

The double-gabled three-storey section of the building provided wards for women on the left side of the plans and men on the right, with the "old" on the ground floor and "able-bodied" on the upper floors. The children's dormitories were situated over the schoolrooms. The main circulation stairs were positioned on each side at the intersection between the two-storey and three-storey blocks, with the optional ventilation tower positioned overhead. The arrangement of the rooms and dormitories portrayed the class order of the workhouses:

from supreme to base morality ... the Guardians were at the very top of this scale. The children's wards were nestled around the Master, safe from contamination around them. The pauper adults, being worse in nature were placed to the extreme wings. The "idiots" were banished to the extreme end of the workhouse because indifferent to right and wrong they presented the greatest moral threat (Thomas 157).

It was forbidden for the various classes of pauper to communicate with one another; even members of families living in close proximity to each other remained separated by impenetrable walls, and the separation of men and women was viewed as a simple and practical method for controlling the population of the poor.

Life in the workhouse was thoroughly regulated and disciplined. The inmates rose at 7 a.m., dressed in rough workhouse clothes, were inspected by the master for cleanliness, then went to the central dining hall, "marching in file to the tables, where was spread the yellow 'stirabout', in tins and pans, measured and meted by ounces and pounds, suited to age and condition" (Nicholson 83). The rules stipulated that they sit in silence on wooden benches, as "any paupers who shall make any noise when silence is ordered to be kept shall be deemed disorderly and shall be punished accordingly" (O'Connor 104).

After breakfast the inmates – including children, the aged and the frail – were put to work. It was a fundamental rule of the workhouse system that no individual capable of physical exertion must ever be permitted to be idle. The able-bodied men's work included breaking stones, grinding corn, and working on the farm. In *Annals of the Famine in Ireland*, Asenath Nicholson describes seeing "a company of ragged and tattered beings of all ages, from the man of gray hairs to the lad in his teens, sitting upon the ground, breaking stones with 'might and main', and piling them in heaps", and seeing elsewhere in the yards "'weaker vessels' standing in groups or squatting upon their heels, with naked arms and feet" (83).

The able-bodied women mended and washed clothes, attended to the children and the sick, and sometimes joined the men breaking stones. A Perrott wheel, for grinding corn, was installed in several Irish workhouses; this Orwellian contraption involved large groups of inmates (up to a hundred) manually and tortuously rotating a large wheel for long periods of time. The aged and infirm women were required to do lighter work, including knitting and spinning wool, as well as making clothes for the inmates. The disabled men worked in the kitchen, along with the women, or carried out light work around the house and yard. All of this was work without incentive, as they received no compensation other than meager board and lodgings for their labor.

The inmates returned to the dormitories at 8 p.m., but leisure time and activities were restricted. All types of card games were prohibited, as was tobacco and alcohol. Any breaches of the rules or failure to work were punished by time in the dismal refractory wards – essentially small cells in which the floor, walls, ceiling, and raised platform bed were constructed entirely of stone, making them permanently cold, damp, and hard. A ballast of rubble stone was placed over the stone ceiling to prevent anyone from lifting out the stone slabs to escape confinement.

The dining hall was located in a single-storey, long, narrow building located behind the dormitory block and centered on the axis of the symmetrical plan. Men, women, and children would access the dining hall at different times and from a series of separate doors to maintain the integrity of segregation. The basic diet and simple menus are well recorded in the masters' journals and records. Typically, the inmates would be served a breakfast of oatmeal and Indian meal with buttermilk, a dinner of potatoes with sweet milk (and very occasionally poor-quality meat), and an evening meal of porridge, bread, and milk. Asenath Nicholson described the diet:

Figure 12 | Infirmary building viewed from the female yard, Portumna Union Workhouse

The "yaller Indian" here, was the dreadful thing that they told me, "swells us and takes the life of us"; and as it was there cooked, it may be scrupled whether any officer in the establishment would select it for his food, though he assured the inmates "he could eat it, and it was quite good enough for a king" (82).

There was little variation in the menu, with the exception of Christmas and midsummer, when sweet-cake might be included. All meals were prepared in the kitchen located between the dining hall and the men's dormitory block.

The laundry was opposite, on the women's side. The dining hall also functioned as a general chapel for all religions. The Commissioners believed that politics and religion were the "two greatest points of contention in Ireland" (Thomas 158), and ruled that workhouses were to be non-denominational and that religious ministers were prohibited from becoming guardians. Politics was strictly forbidden within the workhouses. However, pragmatically, local clergy of various creeds were permitted to conduct religious services and administer to the spiritual needs of the inmates.

The men's and women's yards were situated on either side of the dining hall, surrounded by the dormitory blocks and the infirmary to the rear. The infirmary, located in the third section of the workhouse, was a two-storey building running parallel to the main dormitory structure and located to the rear of the dining hall. The infirmary was designed "to meet the casual sickness arising in a number of inmates generally presumed to be healthy, and in ordinary circumstances they have been usually found proportioned to those requirements" (Poor Law Commission, *Thirteenth Annual Report* 25). It included male and female wards on either side, and a surgery and nurse's room in the center. Male and female wards for "idiots" and "lunatic" cells were positioned at the ends of each wing. To the rear of this block were four separate yards further separating male and female patients and "idiots". Isolated at the rear of the complex was a small mortuary named the Dead House, to which able-bodied inmates brought the corpses of the dead, bringing to an end the cycle of life in the workhouse [Figure 12].

PRACTICAL GEOLOGY AND ANCIENT ARCHITECTURE

During his extensive travels across Ireland, Wilkinson acquired a vast knowledge of local building materials. He also studied and recorded many of the ancient ruins, and published his findings in *Practical Geology and Ancient Architecture of Ireland* (1845). The book includes chapters on ancient architecture, practical geology, and the origins and use of stone in Ireland for building purposes. It is illustrated with his own drawings and woodcuts, demonstrating his considerable skill as an artist and draftsman. He lists the various building stones to be found within each county, and provides tables related to experiments detailing the weight, absorption, cohesion, and resistance to fracture of over six hundred Irish stone types, reflecting his precise, scientific, and practical approach to building.

In his detailed essay "Building on the stones of Ireland: George Wilkinson's *Practical Geology and Ancient Architecture* (1845)", Dr William Taylor observes that Wilkinson's book "On a more philosophical level … outlines an ethical context within which evaluations about 'good' architecture and 'good' people were made in the middle decades of the nineteenth century" (152). Wilkinson's evaluation of "good" architecture proposes that it is "not necessary to refer to the nations of remote antiquity" (*Practical Geology and Ancient Architecture* 5) to find appropriate architectural reference; rather, he encourages Irish architects to look at their own country, where they can find "some enduring monuments of the skill and boldness of design" of their ancestors, and asks "who can contemplate the noble ruins of which meet the eye throughout the country without feeling respect for those who reared the structures, and the laws and institutions under which they were originated?" He also encourages "more general readers to learn the value of remaining in one's local environment, where, surrounded by architecture that suited the geography and history of native lands, they could develop a deeper sense of self and historical awareness" (*Practical Geology and Ancient Architecture* 5), expressing a view that can be seen as consistent with the concerns of the Commissioners, who feared the migratory habit of the Irish. Wilkinson is critical of the poor quality of present-day buildings, saying that *durability of construction and simplicity of design are too commonly disregarded and sacrificed for a pleasing outline, according to the prevalent notions that plaster, cements, or any perishable material is sufficient; the intention being tamely to imitate approved forms, which, however, when applied under different circumstances, produce an inferior effect* (*Practical Geology and Ancient Architecture* 6).

He attributes this failure to produce "good" architecture to the lack of understanding of the benefits brought by trained architects. He calls on Irish architects to share their understanding and promote discourse between professionals and artists, as in England and on the Continent, "whenever the arts and sciences have advanced to any high degree of excellence" (*Practical Geology and Ancient Architecture* 152). *Practical Geology and Ancient Architecture of Ireland* is clearly intended to promote Wilkinson's career and status in Ireland; he asks for acceptance as an Englishman in Ireland, just as "in England some of the most elevated and honoured positions, with regard to the fine arts, are persons of Irish birth" (*Practical Geology and Ancient Architecture* 153); this probably refers to the likes of William Mulready RA (1786–1863) and Daniel Maclise (1806–70), both of whom were highly regarded in London's artistic circles.

For building, Wilkinson encourages the use of local materials – particularly quarried stone – making an argument for their economic benefits: "not only would the employment of people be greatly and profitably extended, but much wealth now commonly leaving the country, might be expected to be retained in it" (*Practical Geology and Ancient Architecture* 10). His views resonate with those of Whately and O'Connell, who had proposed public-works projects for the relief of the poor.

Although many of his contemporaries held prejudiced views of the Irish as a hopeless, backward, and impoverished race, Wilkinson envisaged a more positive outlook for the future of the Irish if they could recover a sense of ownership of the ancient culture of their ancestors, achieve a sense of belonging and place, and identify with the "noble memorials of a vigorous and powerful race" (*Practical Geology and Ancient Architecture* 117). Taylor suggests that these comments "resonate distantly with sentiments shared by the Young Ireland movement in the 1840s aimed at asserting the linguistic, cultural, and historical identity of the Irish" (156).

Wilkinson's empathy with the Irish fails to extend to the condition of the poor and the victims of the workhouse system. He makes only one reference to the plight of the poor: "perhaps no country in the world presents a more wretched class of buildings than the houses in which the majority of the population reside" (*Practical Geology and Ancient Architecture* 150). *Practical Geology and Ancient Architecture of Ireland* was written in 1845, before the Famine had struck, but clearly shows that he was conscious of the atrocious living conditions suffered by the poor. He was a government agent gainfully employed and fully committed to the delivery of the workhouse buildings, and unlikely to publish anything that would compromise his position. His approach to the design of workhouses was entirely technical, and he was never seen to question their devastating social implications. His middle-class views reflected his own position in society, and he accepted unquestioningly the place and prospects of the poor. His commentary on Irish culture was shaped by concern for his own future prospects and career following the workhouse commission, and he displayed little of the compassion reflected in Thomas Noel's lines:

> *You bumpkin, who stare at your brother conveyed;*
> *Behold what respect to a cloddy is paid,*
> *And be joyful to think, when death you're laid low,*
> *You've a chance to the grave like a genman to go.*
> *"Rattle his bones over the stones;*
> *He's only a pauper, whom nobody owns!"*

GRIM BASTILLES OF DESPAIR – CONTEMPORARY CRITICISM

In *Tales from the Poorhouse*, a suite of monologues based on the fictional lives of workhouse inmates, the master, and a landlord, Eugene McCabe imagines a conversation between Wilkinson and a wealthy landlord:

6 April 1848
Called at the poorhouse again. Murphy still hiding away. Sounds less unhinged. Put my head into the yard privies on the way out. Even a thousand paupers shat there today they shouldn't smell so foul. Crap pits could have been built over barrows for dragging straight to fields. Romans doing that before Christ, the Chinese before that. Wilkinson's fault. Wretched, puffed up architect.
– Clearing them out will give them something to do, he said.
Shoddy jobwork. No imagination. I implied as much last time he was here.
– Would you like a paupers' billiard hall, my Lord? A ballroom? A few tennis courts? A croquet lawn perhaps?
Touchy man. Went on to say the first poorhouses in England were designed as houses of terror, and that John Russell, the PM himself, had admired "the humane and frugal grace" of his plans.
– It would be difficult, I said, to imagine anything more frugal. I could have added, "Or more inhuman".
He noted that. Swilling down my claret, apropos of nothing he said,
– What ruins most landscapes from here to Moscow are these brute erections with their balls up on gatepillars shouting: "Behold me, little people! See my big windows, my big door, my ice-house, my artificial lake!" Makes for bad architecture and worse politics!
After quite a silence I asked,
– Would you include Versailles?
– In particular Versailles.
– Its gardens?
– Worse again.
What gardens, I asked, did he most admire?
– Any cottier's vegetable patch, anywhere.
Tin-made spouting. Middle-class jealousy. What the French revolution was mostly about.

Won't eat with me again. His plans used all over Ireland. The outskirts of every other town. Grim bastilles of despair. Imagines himself a radical reformer. An obtuse idiot. Could have, but didn't, return rudeness for rudeness (75–6).

This fictional account expresses an Irish landlord's criticism of the design and management of the workhouses, and also declares Wilkinson's middle-class views of the Irish gentry. In real life the appearance of workhouse buildings had at the time been denounced by many critics for being stark and ugly, and the gray stone walls were compared to prison walls. These criticisms upset Wilkinson, as can be seen in his report of 1847:

It may not be an unimportant matter for me further to remark on the want of greater attention to the workhouse sites of most of the Unions and in the proper cultivation of land, and the arrangement of paths and roadways around the workhouses. In some Unions where individual Guardians have taken an interest in these matters, or where there has been an intelligent and active workhouse master, the ground is well cultivated, the roadways and paths are carefully formed and well covered with broken stones or gravel, the open drains are kept clear, the outer-yard walls are being covered with ivy or other creepers, and neat shrubs, evergreens, or trees contribute to give a cheerful and inviting appearance to the establishment occasioning it, with much advantage to the institutions, to be visited and inspected by the inhabitants of the Union, and a warm interest to be frequently taken by visitors in the welfare of the inmates and the good management of the institution, instead of its being rendered repulsive, as is sometimes the case, by the appearance or neglect of its external features (Poor Law Commission, *Thirteenth Annual Report* 137).

The physical construction of the workhouses had also been criticized. Several Boards of Guardians complained to the Commissioners regarding problems of supervision, delays with contractors, and poor-quality workmanship. These issues arose from the fact that Wilkinson had sole responsibility for the design and erection of the buildings while the funds for their construction were supplied by the Boards of Guardians of the various Poor Law Unions; "it would be no matter of surprise", Wilkinson noted, "that operations conducted under such circumstances should be attended with endless jealousies, and with difficulties greatly increased by the necessity of conciliating the various opinions and different views, as well as reconciling the conflicting interests, of local parties" (Poor Law Commission, *Thirteenth Annual Report* 153). The extent of complaints was sufficient to warrant a series of official investigations, the first of which was carried out by Jacob Owen, who – not surprisingly, having developed a close professional and personal relationship with Wilkinson – found little wrong.

Further complaints prompted a second investigation, this time conducted by James Pennethorne (1801–71), a London-based architect. He arrived on October 9, 1843 and published a critical report in 1844, in which he concluded that "the appointment of only one architect to superintend and to conduct the erection of 130 workhouses spread all over Ireland was most mistaken economy", and added that there was careless workmanship and faulty design, and that "disasters were sure to occur from such hasty proceedings and the adoption of plans so little preconsidered as to detail" (24). He acknowledged Wilkinson's hard work, but blamed him for not pointing out likely problems to the guardians. Criticism was not solely directed at the architect but also at the Commissioners. Nicholls was furious; he lambasted Pennethorne for the report, and strongly defended Wilkinson in a published letter (dated June 16, 1844) addressed to the home secretary, Sir James Graham.

It must have been irritating for Wilkinson to find his professionalism challenged by a London-based gentleman architect, especially as Pennethorne had failed to consult with him during the course of his investigations. Wilkinson defended his approach to building the workhouses in a two-page section of his book *Practical Geology and Ancient Architecture of Ireland*:

the particulars of ... [the report], strange to say, were only known to those assailed on their appearing in print, who were afforded no opportunity of explanation before their promulgation, and who were afterwards limited to a time so circumscribed as not to admit of any fair or complete exposition of the facts by which the statements of the report would have been controverted in detail (155).

Pennethorne was not incorrect in his criticism, but because his views conflicted with those of Owen's initial report, in 1845 the government established a third inquiry, this time under Lieutenant Colonel George Barney of the Royal Engineers. His report provided a more balanced view of the merits and shortcomings of the designs. He was nevertheless "inclined to consider that economy has been carried to an extreme not desirable in public buildings where durability becomes a leading and important consideration" (13).

Even though this failure contradicts Wilkinson's own published views on the durability of the construction, he managed to weather the storm of criticism – partly due to the success of his book – and maintained his position as the Commissioners' architect. However, in response to the criticism he made various changes in the design of the workhouses – changes that might otherwise not have occurred. These changes included improvements to the ventilation system and prevention of damp ingress by the introduction of a rendered finish to the façades.

HUNGER WILL BREAK THROUGH A STONE WALL: IMPACT OF THE FAMINE

The workhouses had not been designed to alleviate mass starvation and famine; nor does it seem to have been a consideration, given that Nicholls shared Malthus's view that famine was a necessary means for controlling the population. In 1836 Nicholls stated that "the occurrence of a famine, if general, seems to be a contingency altogether above the powers of the poor law to provide for" (38). Many workhouses had been only half full before the Famine, but by 1846, soon after the potato crop failed, a number of them were already full.

Before the famine they were many of them quite interesting objects for a stranger to visit, generally kept clean, not crowded, and the food sufficient. But when famine advanced, when funds decreased, when the doors were besieged by imploring applicants, who wanted a place to die, that they might be buried in a coffin, they were little else than charnel houses, while the living, shivering skeletons that squatted upon the floors, or stood with arms folded against the wall, half-clad, with hair uncombed, hands and face unwashed, added a horror if not terror to the sight (Nicholson 82).

As the impact of the Famine increased, the numbers seeking relief rose rapidly, and soon many workhouses were dealing with as many as three times their planned number.

There are in Nenagh Union Workhouse at present between seven hundred and eight hundred persons, the number is augmenting every week; and with the present prospects, we should not wonder if the house were crowded beyond the number for which it was built, namely one thousand, within three or four weeks. Meanwhile, starvation presents its fearful appearance in many districts; and the wail of despair is commencing to be heard (*The Vindicator*, October 25, 1846).[3]

The workhouses were forced to make various emergency modifications in an attempt to cope with the growing numbers. However, the Commissioners remained determined to maintain the basic principles underpinning them, being still strongly of the opinion that workhouse accommodation should be reserved for able-bodied persons and their families. They insisted that all additional accommodation should be provided within the workhouse to avoid the necessity of giving outdoor relief. The Commissioners issued a circular recommending Wilkinson's best models for extending buildings; these included extending the wing buildings (most easily achieved on the front building), adding floors, and converting the sheds located next to the infirmary and adjacent to the side walls of the yards for use as dormitories. They also proposed the provision of new wooden sheds – "fever sheds" – that were to function as convalescent space for fever victims. Schoolrooms were also converted to dormitories, with the effect that schooling was dramatically reduced and classes often held in the open yards or in auxiliary buildings outside the complex. Ultimately, these haphazard modifications destroyed Nicholls's vision of a network of identical workhouses throughout the island.

Even with these modifications, many workhouses were unable to cope with the increased numbers, and auxiliary accommodation had to be found outside the workhouse complex. Nearby buildings were leased to accommodate the rapidly increasing numbers; the principle of segregation was maintained, with males and females sent to different buildings. Conditions in these auxiliary buildings – often no more than converted sheds and stores – were generally unhealthy and unhygienic. The outsourcing of accommodation created logistical and financial problems for the guardians, as they now had to raise additional funds to pay for leases and to feed the growing number of inmates. It was inevitable that the cost of food would rise as it became scarcer and harder to acquire, putting the unions under even greater strain.

Maintaining discipline in auxiliary accommodation located outside the workhouses was an additional challenge for the guardians. The auxiliary buildings were generally unsupervised, and it often proved difficult to get the inmates to return each day to work in the main buildings. In an online publication, "Desperate haven: the Famine in Dungarvan", William Fraher describes how, out of 350 inmates who had been moved to a converted store in the town, no more than 140 or 150 returned each day to the main house to work, and how fevered inmates would often wander about the town in their dirty rags, causing great distress among the townspeople regarding the spread of disease.

As the numbers rose, the guardians could no longer afford to clothe or provide bedding for the new inmates, and it was reported that the people worst affected by disease were those who had been allowed to retain their own clothes on entering the workhouse and who had no proper bedding. Many of those seeking relief were half naked on arrival at the workhouses, and often the unclean clothes of diseased dead were passed on to them.

The workhouses in the poorest unions suffered the dual problem of having the least resources to fund changes, and they also tended to have the highest number of destitute. In reality a great many of those seeking relief were turned away, often as a result of the infamous Gregory Clause, a provision of the new relief measures passed under the Irish Poor Law Extension Act in June 1847. This provision exempted from relief anyone who owned more than a quarter of an acre of land. The clause was widely misinterpreted, and some who should have qualified for relief were refused. Many of the more unscrupulous landlords used the Gregory Clause as an excuse to evict thousands of unwanted tenants from their estates, and those made homeless by these evictions were forced to emigrate or seek relief in the workhouses.

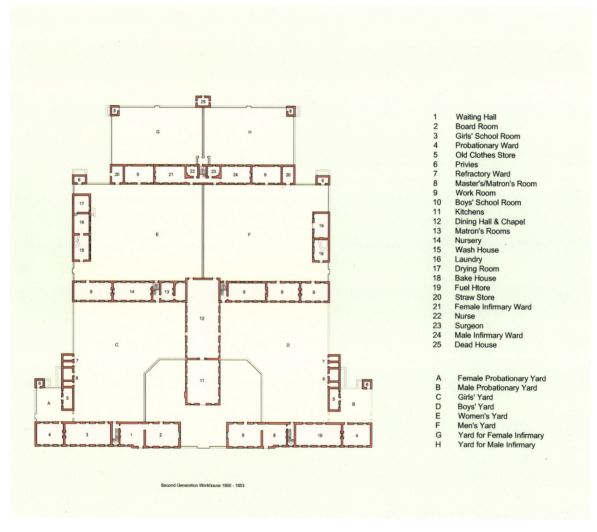

Second Generation Workhouse 1850 - 1853

1	Waiting Hall
2	Board Room
3	Girls' School Room
4	Probationary Ward
5	Old Clothes Store
6	Privies
7	Refractory Ward
8	Master's/Matron's Room
9	Work Room
10	Boys' School Room
11	Kitchens
12	Dining Hall & Chapel
13	Matron's Rooms
14	Nursery
15	Wash House
16	Laundry
17	Drying Room
18	Bake House
19	Fuel Htore
20	Straw Store
21	Female Infirmary Ward
22	Nurse
23	Surgeon
24	Male Infirmary Ward
25	Dead House

A	Female Probationary Yard
B	Male Probationary Yard
C	Girls' Yard
D	Boys' Yard
E	Women's Yard
F	Men's Yard
G	Yard for Female Infirmary
H	Yard for Male Infirmary

Figure 13 | Ground-floor plan, second-generation workhouse

SECOND PHASE OF WORKHOUSES

The completion of the original 130 workhouses coincided, more or less, with the beginning of the Famine, and soon after their completion the Commissioners determined that additional unions would have to be formed in locations with the greatest numbers of destitute. Wilkinson was retained to prepare new workhouse plans for this second phase of unions. His new design was in essence a modification of the earlier buildings: a similar cruciform plan but around larger courtyards, with the laundry, refractory wards, and privies placed to the sides. The small central front building was omitted and replaced with two larger buildings set apart from each other, with the dining hall/chapel set back but visible between them. The two front buildings were two-storey structures containing, at ground level, the master's and matron's accommodation, waiting room, day room, boardroom, boys' schoolroom (right side) and girls' schoolroom (left side), as well as probationary wards, which had their own small yards at each end **[Figure 13]**. The children's dormitories and additional quarters for the master were located on the first-floor level.

The central building contained the kitchen and provided a larger dining hall/chapel, with a bell tower positioned centrally over the roof. The flagstone-floored hall had separate doors opening to each of the male, female, boys' and girls' yards, all of which were segregated from each other by high stone walls and the buildings **[Figure 14]**.

Two refractory wards (in reality solitary-confinement cells) were positioned on the perimeter wall of both the boys' and girls' yard, strategically located next to the privies and cesspool. It is not difficult to imagine the brutality and discomfort of

isolation within these cold, foul-smelling stone rooms, and the impact this would have had on the spirit of already broken people **[Figure 15]**.

The male and female dormitories were accommodated on the upper floors of the three-storey buildings that ran perpendicular to the dining hall, with the able-bodied, infirm, and aged placed in separate wards on different floors. Workrooms, a nursery, and the matron's room were provided at ground level and opened onto the male and female yards to the rear of these buildings, ensuring no uncontrolled contact between the adults and children. The laundry was located in a separate building accessed from the female yard. This small but technically complex building included a drying room raised above the semi-basement furnace, which was positioned under a thin flagstone floor supported on cast-iron rails. A similar-sized bakery building was accessed from the male yard.

The two-storey infirmary building was located at the rear of the male and female yards, and was similar in scale to the first-phase building. However, the "idiot cells" were no longer provided, and a separate fever hospital was generally located in an area isolated from the main workhouse structures. The Dead House was again placed at the far end of the infirmary yards; however, the cemetery was no longer contained within the complex, and was now positioned well away from the buildings.

In response to criticism of the construction, several details of the original buildings were modified, including the application of render to the façades to improve damp resistance, and the installation of timber windows – to achieve better sealing – as replacements for the cast-iron fittings used in the earlier workhouses. The ventilation system for the dormitories was improved by the introduction of a system of timber ducts to channel fresh air under the floor and distribute it via air vents running the length of the sleeping platforms.

As the numbers entering workhouses rose, so did the occurrence of disease and death. Managing the increased numbers put the guardians and masters under great strain, and many workhouses failed to maintain the necessary standards of hygiene. Insufficient cleaning, maintenance, and whitewashing of the interiors, defective ventilation, and poor quality of food (so bad at times that even the starving could not eat it), had disastrous consequences, with disease reaching epidemic proportions and the number of deaths multiplying. The dead had originally been buried in well-managed plots within the grounds of the workhouse, but as the numbers grew and good management failed, many of the dead were buried in mass graves within yards of buildings, where the rats "can feast there for a hundred years! And keep away from the living, Sir, the half living, and half dying" (McCabe 93). These ill-considered burial pits were often in poorly chosen locations, thereby causing contamination of the water supply and the inevitable spread of even more disease.

Figure 15 | Refractory ward, Kilmacthomas Union Workhouse

The average annual figure for deaths within the workhouses before the Famine had been just under five thousand, but that number increased considerably during the Famine years, as recorded in the 1851 census of Ireland.

Average annual workhouse deaths. *Source: 1851 census of Ireland*	
1846	14,662
1847	68,900
1848	45,482
1849	64,440
1850	46,721
1851	38,000

Almost a third of a million people died in the workhouses during the Famine, and in the worst years – 1847–49 – up to one in four inmates died. Of the one million who died during the Famine, one in four died in workhouses, leading to one workhouse being described as "little more than a charnel house" (MacAtaseney 167).

As the Famine began to wane in 1850–51, so, too, did the numbers entering the workhouses. The pressure on the buildings and the guardians abated with the drop in the numbers of destitute. The increasing association of disease and death with the workhouses magnified the resolve of the poor to avoid these institutions. During the following decades, most workhouses were adapted for use as hospitals, and became the backbone of the Irish hospital system. Many remain in use as hospitals, where the sick and aged are attended to within their historic walls, most of them oblivious as to their dark legacy and the unnamed ghosts of the forgotten poor.

NOTE ON GEORGE WILKINSON

Wilkinson's role as architect to the Irish Commissioners continued until 1855, by which time he had already set up a private practice. In 1850 he returned briefly to Witney to marry Mary Clinch, but he remained in Ireland for the rest of his professional career, where he "found comfort from the accusations made by his native country" (Quinn 68). Quinn, in ""Perspectives on the career of George Wilkinson", suggests that it is a testament to his character that he was accepted in Irish society "despite having covered the Irish landscape with one of the most despised monuments to British dominance" (74). It appears that he was an amicable person and well liked by those who knew him. He also cared about gaining the respect of his fellow professionals, and was keen to embrace Irish society. He was a member of the Royal Irish Academy, the Royal Zoological Society, and the Geological Society of Dublin, and immersed himself in academic, scientific, and literary scenes, giving lectures based on the findings recounted in his book. In 1842 he was elected onto the Royal Institute of the Architects of Ireland council, and served as vice-president from 1864 to 1868. It is interesting to note that in 1863 he proposed "that a new president be selected from among the profession, and not as heretofore elected from the aristocracy" (Quinn 49), thereby removing a potential "class" obstacle for the promotion of an ambitious regional architect.

During his later career he designed a number of railway stations, including the Dublin, Wicklow & Wexford terminus at Harcourt Street, Dublin (opened in 1859). From 1860 to 1886 he was architect for the Commissioners of Asylums for the Lunatic Poor, for which body he designed two identical asylums at Castlebar, County Mayo and Letterkenny, County Donegal. His last important recorded commission was the new agricultural hall for the Royal Dublin Society at Ballsbridge, built 1879–80. In 1887 he returned to England, where he died at Ryde House in Twickenham on October 4, 1890. And so he went – like the hundreds of thousands unnamed who inhabited his workhouses – "Naked and lonely into the ground" (McCabe 47).[4]

ENDNOTES

1 Daniel O'Connell, parliamentary debate, 1838, quoted in O'Connor, *The Workhouses of Ireland*, 65.

2 George Nicholls, letter to John Shaw-Lefevre, April 8, 1839, quoted in Quinn,"Perspectives on the Career of George Wilkinson", 44.

3 Letter from Cornelius O'Brien, October 25, 1846, published in *The Vindicator* (Belfast), October 31, 1846.

4 This an adaptation of Thomas Noel's poem.

WORKS CITED

Barney, George. *Report of the Commissioner Appointed to Inquire into the Execution of the Contracts for Certain Union Workhouses in Ireland*. London: 1845.

Burke, Helen. *The People and the Poor Law in 19th Century Ireland*. Dublin: 1987.

Dallat, Cahal. *Caring by Design*. Belfast: Department of Health and Social Services, 1985.

de Beaumont, Gustave. *Ireland, Social Political and Religious.* London: 1839

Dickens, Charles. *Oliver Twist*. Ware, Hertfordshire: Wordsworth, 2000.

Dictionary of Irish Architects. Irish Architectural Archive: http://www.dia.ie.

Fraher, William. "Desperate haven: the Famine in Dungarvan". Waterford County Museum, online publication. http://www.waterfordmuseum.ie/exhibit/web/Display/article/330/21/Desperate_Haven_The_Famine_in_Dungarvan_Famine_Graveyards_.html.

MacAtasney, Gerard. "Lurgan workhouse". *Atlas of the Great Irish Famine*. Eds. John Crowley, William J. Smyth, and Mike Murphy. Cork: Cork University Press, 2012.

McCabe, Eugene. *Tales from the Poorhouse*. Oldcastle, County Meath: Gallery Press, 1999.

Nicholls, George. *First Annual Report on Poor Laws in Ireland*. London: 1836.

Nicholson, Asenath. *Annals of the Irish Famine, in 1847, 1848 and 1849.* New York: E. French, 1851.

O'Connor, John. *The Workhouses of Ireland: The Fate of Ireland's Poor.* Dublin: Anvil Books, 1995.

O'Dwyer, Frederick. *Irish Hospital Architecture: A Pictorial History*. Dublin: Department of Health and Children, 1997.

Pennethorne, James. *Report of Royal Commission Appointed to Inquire into the Execution of the Contracts for Certain Union Workhouses in Ireland*. London: 1844.

Poor Law Commission. *Fifth Annual Report of the Poor Law Commissioners: With Appendices*. London: 1839.

---. *Seventh Annual Report of the Poor Law Commissioners: With Appendices*. London: 1841.

---. *Twelfth Annual Report of the Poor Law Commissioners: With Appendices.* London: 1846.

---. *Thirteenth Annual Report of the Poor Law Commissioners: With Appendices.* London: 1847.

Quinn, Beth-Anne. "Perspectives on the career of George Wilkinson: workhouse architect in England and Ireland", 2 vols, vol. 1. MA thesis. University College, Dublin, 1997.

Taylor, Dr William. "Building on the stones of Ireland: George Wilkinson's *Practical Geology and Ancient Architecture* (1845)". *Études Irlandaises* 30.1 (2005).

Thomas, Liz. "Ulster workhouses: ideological geometry and conflict". *Atlas of the Great Irish Famine*. Eds. John Crowley, William J. Smyth, and Mike Murphy. Cork: Cork University Press, 2012.

Wilkinson, George. *Specification of Works Required to be Performed in the Erection of the Union Workhouses.* Dublin: Alexander Thom, 1839.

---. *Practical Geology and Ancient Architecture of Ireland*. London and Dublin: John Murray and William Curry, 1845.

IMAGES

Cover
Francis William Topham
1808–77
Feeding Chickens
1848
Watercolor
15.75 x 11.42 in (40 x 29 cm)
© Ireland's Great Hunger
Museum, Quinnipiac University

Figure 1
"Group of Cabins at Ardcara"
Pictorial Times
January 31, 1846
Image provided by Ireland's
Great Hunger Museum,
Quinnipiac University

Figure 2
Portumna Union Workhouse
Photograph by Paschal
Mahoney

Figure 3
Ramsay Richard Reinagle
1775–1862
Sir George Nicholls
Oil on canvas
36.125 x 32.125 in (91.8 x 81.6 cm)
1834
NPG 4807
© National Portrait Gallery,
London

Figure 4
Photograph of George
Wilkinson
Royal Institute of the Architects
of Ireland

Figure 5
George Wilkinson
1814–90
Bird's eye view of workhouse to
contain 400 to 800 persons
Poor Law Commission. *Fifth
Annual Report of the Poor
Law Commissioners: With
Appendices.*
London: 1839
Image provided by Irish
Architectural Archive

Figure 6
George Wilkinson
1814–90
Interior view of the workhouse
building, showing the
construction and arrangement
of the sleeping platforms and
bedsteads
Image provided by Irish
Architectural Archive

Figure 7
View to stairs from dormitory,
Portumna Union Workhouse
Photograph by Rowan Dowling-
Mahoney

Figure 8
George Wilkinson
1814–90
Part of drawing showing detail
of ventilator over main stairs,
Mallow Union Workhouse
Image provided by Irish
Architectural Archive

Figure 9
George Wilkinson
1814–90
Section drawing through
dormitory building, Portumna
Union Workhouse
Image provided by Irish
Architectural Archive

Figure 10
Ground-floor plan, first-
generation workhouse
Drawing by Paschal Mahoney

Figure 11
Dormitory sleeping platforms,
Portumna Union Workhouse
Photograph by Rowan Dowling-
Mahoney

Figure 12
Infirmary building viewed from
the female yard, Portumna
Union Workhouse
Photograph by Rowan Dowling-
Mahoney

Figure 13
Ground-floor plan, second-
generation workhouse
Drawing by Paschal Mahoney

Figure 14
View of the female dormitory
and dining hall/chapel from
girls' yard, Donaghmore Union
Workhouse
Photograph by Rowan Dowling-
Mahoney

Figure 15
Refractory ward, Kilmacthomas
Union Workhouse
Photograph by Paschal Mahoney

ABOUT THE AUTHOR

Paschal Mahoney is an architect in private practice based in Dublin. He graduated from University College, Dublin in 1987, and was elected a Member of the Royal Institute of the Architects of Ireland (RIAI) in 1990, and a Fellow of the RIAI in 2016. He has worked in London, Moscow, and Dublin, and in 1998 established Mahoney Architecture. He has worked on several projects involving the conservation and reimagining of workhouses.

ACKNOWLEDGMENTS

My deep appreciation and sincere thanks to Niamh O'Sullivan and Luke Gibbons for their guidance and for kindly sharing their great knowledge and insight. To my inspiration, Rachael Dowling, for her unwavering support and constant encouragement, and to my son, Rowan Dowling-Mahoney, for his patience and good company on field trips, and for his excellent photographic images featured in this folio. Thanks also to my colleagues at Mahoney Architecture, especially Elaine Mahoney-McCabe, Fergus Devine, Dan Balosanu (photo editing and graphics), and Tom Walsh (graphics).

I would also like to acknowledge the kind assistance of Trevor Stanley, Donaghmore Union Workhouse and Agricultural Museum; Stephen Dolan, Portumna Union Workhouse, National Workhouse Museum; and Niall Barry, Kilmacthomas Union Workhouse, for allowing me to access and photograph these buildings.

IRELAND'S GREAT HUNGER MUSEUM | QUINNIPIAC UNIVERSITY PRESS ©2016

SERIES EDITORS

Niamh O'Sullivan
Grace Brady

IMAGE RESEARCH

Claire Puzarne

DESIGN

Rachel Foley

ACKNOWLEDGMENT

Office of Public Affairs, Quinnipiac University

PUBLISHER

Quinnipiac University Press

PRINTING

GRAPHYCEMS

ISBN 978-0-9978374-2-1

Ireland's Great Hunger Museum
Quinnipiac University

3011 Whitney Avenue
Hamden, CT 06518-1908
203-582-6500

www.ighm.org